MAKING FACES

A COMPLETE GUIDE TO FACE PAINTING

SIAN ELLIS-THOMAS

CHARTWELL
BOOKS, INC.

Published by
CHARTWELL BOOKS, INC.
A Division of BOOK SALES, INC.
P.O. Box 7100
114 Northfield Avenue,
Edison, New Jersey 08818-7100

© Revelation Publishing Ltd 1996

Designer: Blackjacks
Photography: Alex Morton and Sian Ellis-Thomas

ISBN 0 7858 0640 7

Printed and bound in China

CONTENTS

ACKNOWLEDGEMENTS

The Publishers and Author would like to thank the following people for their contributions to the production

THE MODELS
Larry and Luke Newman, Paula and Elisabeth Higgins, Helen and Elisabeth Hilton, Jazz Senior, James and Anna Ede, Kirsty and Tammy Morris, James, Jason and Jodie Ellis, Steve and Tommy Dixon, Vicki Lee, Matthew Peet, Rohan "Catman".

Special thanks to:-
Kryolan Corporation, Charles Fox Ltd, Revelation Film Group, Nigel Blundell, Hanne Pedersen, David Ellis-Thomas, Davo the Clown, Jo Mountain, Debbie Burrows, Ann Kendall, Oli Ellis-Thomas, Adele Ede.

STOCKISTS

All the make up and accessories used throughout this book are from the Kryolan -Aquacolor range. The following outlets stock the Aquacolor range of face painting products and are also available by mail order. Alternatively you can try your local theatrical or fancy dress shop.

Australia	**New Zealand**	**UK**	**USA**
Backstage Theatrical	Costume Magic	Charles H. Fox Ltd	Kryolan Corporation
Shop 12, Upper Plaza	1 Howe Street	22 Tavistock Street	132 9th Street
95 Bourke Street	PO Box 86 384	Covent Garden	San Francisco
Melbourne, Vic 3000	Newton	London WC2E 7PY	CA 94103
TEL: 6544147	TEL: 09-3663003	TEL : 0171 240 3111	USA
FAX: 6547696	FAX: 09-3663033	FAX : 0171 379 3410	TEL : 415 863 9684
			FAX : 415 863 9059
John Wurzel & Co.	Minifies Make Up	Making Faces	
PTY Ltd	PO Box 5317	390 Stanstead Road	
Beauty and Pharmacy	194 Wairakei Road	London	
Supplies	Christchurch 5	SE6 4XB	
1201 Glenhuntly Road	Tel: 3519224	TEL : 0181 690 0739	
Glenhuntly, 3163 Vic			
TEL: 5722203			
FAX: 57186658			

**Also available on video: Making Faces – A Guide To Face Painting
PAR 50031 (Paradox Films Ltd, 5 & 6 Parkside, Ravenscourt Park, London W6 0UU)**

INTRODUCTION

Welcome to the wonderful world of face painting. Making faces is not new, it's been around in some form or another for centuries. Body decoration has been and still is used all over the world for all kinds of purposes. From clowns to kabuki, punk rockers to princesses, people have been dressing up and putting on make-up since time began: for ceremonies, in theatre, and of course just for fun! And that's what face painting is all about – fun.

Like most professional face painters, I stumbled across it quite by chance. I began painting my children's faces and enjoyed it so much that I decided to give up my job and take up face painting full time. Not knowing where to go for advice, I just picked up a brush and started to paint, learning the hard way.

Remembering those early attempts, I cringe with embarrassment but just like everything you learn, the more you do the better you get, and in this case practice really does make perfect!

Four years (and a lot of practice) later I'm still having fun.

Face painting is a wonderful skill to have and can bring great happiness to young and old alike. Every face painter I have ever met has a story to melt your heart. The look on a child's face, whether you've transformed them into a beautiful princess or a ferocious tiger, is a picture of joy to treasure always. Face painting is a must at fundraising events and always goes down a storm at parties. Before you know it you'll be the most popular person in the room, so don't be surprised when your services are suddenly in constant demand.

I hope you enjoy this book and that it sparks off a long-term (and probably incurable!) addiction to this very special art.

Happy face painting

Sian Ellis-Thomas

EQUIPMENT

As in any job, before you start you need the right equipment, and in order to make the right decision before you buy you need to know a little more about the different kinds of make-up available. There are two basic types of make-up, oil based – or grease paint, as it is often called – and water based or Aquacolor.

OIL-BASED MAKE-UP

Oil-based make-up is used in theatre, tv, films and fashion. Once it is applied it is then set with a special fixing powder to make it last for many hours, sometimes under extreme conditions of heat, light and even underwater. It takes a lot of skill to apply and has to be removed with an oil-based lotion or cream.

WATER-BASED MAKE UP

Water-based make-up (for example Aquacolor) is used less frequently in the theatre and tv but can be just as long lasting under the right circumstances. It's far easier to apply than its oily relative and infinitely easier to remove. So for face painting purposes and especially for children, water-based make-up is the best and safest thing to use. Ordinary soap, water and a flannel will remove water-based paints.

WHAT YOU NEED

PAINT

Face paints are readily available and come in a huge variety of colours and shades including metallic, pearlised and fluorescent. To get you started you can get a palette of 6 or 12 colours.

As your confidence increases so will your demand for new colours.

Below is a suggested list of colours, use it as a starting point until you develop your own preferences. You will soon get to know which colours you use most often and therefore which to buy in the larger, more economical sizes.

1. WHITE
2. BLACK
3. YELLOW
4. RED
5. BLUE
6. GREEN
7. ORANGE
8. PINK
9. PALE BLUE
10. LILAC
11. PURPLE
12. SILVER
13. BRIGHT PINK
14. BROWN
15. GOLD
16. PALE GREEN
17. LIGHT BROWN
18. SEA GREEN
19. DARK RED
20. BRICK RED

BRUSHES

As with all skills you are only as good as your tools allow, so it pays to invest in some good quality brushes. Sable brushes are considered the best and of course are the most expensive, but for face painting, inexpensive ox-hair and even some good acrylic types will do the job just as well.

There are literally hundreds of different shapes and sizes available and as you progress you will develop your own preferences, but to start with choose two or three brushes. The most useful would be a medium round (number 6) large flat (half inch) and a fine round or flat (number 2). All the faces in this book can be achieved using these three brushes.

SPONGES

Make up sponges are essential for face painting if you want to achieve a quick, even base and successful blending. There are

various sponges available on the market but the best ones to use are fine acrylic make-up sponges. These can be used whole or cut into halves or quarters for easy handling and also for economy! A stipple sponge is also worth investing in to create beard stubble and other texture effects.

You will also need several bowls of water for the sponges and brushes, some small paint pots for mixing the paints, plus a supply of tissues, wet wipes, hairbands, hairgrips and a mirror.

MAINTENANCE

The main point to remember with all your equipment is that the more you take care of it the longer it will last. The paints should be wiped clean after each session, the lids replaced and then stored in a dry place. Rinse your brushes out after use and clean them with a mild detergent. It is also a good idea to give them a good soak in a fabric or hair conditioner to prevent them drying

out. When they are clean and dry a tiny dab of moisturising cream on the tip of each brush will also add to their lifespan. Sponges should be rinsed out thoroughly after each session and then washed with your usual washing detergent. An overnight soak in a biological stain remover will also help keep them looking bright. With this extra care your equipment will last a lot longer.

EXTRAS

There are a number of extras you can use for face painting. These are not essential items but will certainly help to make your job easier, quicker and more effective.

☆ Glitter creme.
☆ Blusher and brush.
☆ Lipstick.
☆ Theatre blood.
☆ Cosmetic stars and jewels.
☆ Water-based theatre glue (spirit gum).
☆ Cake make-up bases. These are exactly as they suggest: a base over which other make up can be applied. They are a powder formulation and are applied in the same way as face paint using a damp sponge. Available in a range of skin tones and black and white they are very useful for face painting, especially as a base for dark skins and as a substitute for a white paint base on any skin.

WHERE TO GET SUPPLIES

You can buy your face paints and accessories from theatrical make-up shops, some chain-store retailers and fancydress shops. The Aquacolor face paints used in this book are manufactured by Kryolan. A list of their stockists appears at the back of this book.

PREPARATION

Have all your equipment laid out on a table within easy reach. It's a good idea to cover your work table with a plastic cloth which can be wiped clean.

Decide whether you will paint standing up with your model sitting down, or sitting in a chair opposite your model. Whichever way you choose, take care not to strain your back with bad posture and unnecessary stretching and twisting. It helps to keep your working area clean, so have a carrier bag or waste bin under the table to discard used wet wipes, tissues and so on.

Tell your model what you are going to do before you paint and give reassurance while you are painting. If necessary keep the model's hair off the face with a clip or hairband (tell the boys it's a sweatband if they're embarrassed).

Star Tips

Throughout the book look out for the Star Tips. These are the extra little professional hints picked up over years of face painting that help to turn an O.K. face into a K.O. face!

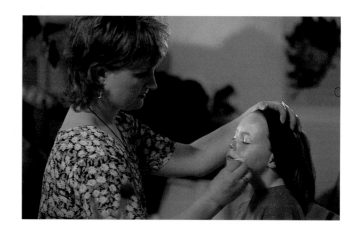

FACE PAINTERS' CODE OF PRACTICE

☆ Always use professional paints and products recommended for face painting.

☆ Do not paint a child with an apparent skin disorder or allergy. If in doubt do a patch test on the inside of the wrist before you paint the face. If there is no reaction after an hour it should be safe to proceed.

☆ Always use clean utensils. Wash containers, brushes and sponges thoroughly after each session and keep them clean during the session.

☆ Change brush water frequently.

☆ Be extra careful when painting near the eyes, especially on very young children and those

unable to keep still.

☆ Never add disinfectant to the water.

☆ If you intend to paint faces in the public domain you are advised to have public liabilty insurance cover.

These are simple guidelines advised by FACE – the U.K. Face Painting Association, to help painters work in a safe and hygienic condition and to protect them and the faces they paint. Anyone interested in finding out more about FACE should write to FACE, Rookery Barn, Sandpit Lane, Bledlow. Bucks. HP27 9QQ

TECHNIQUES

APPLYING A BASE

☆ Always start with a clean dry face (look out for runny noses and oily hair products).

☆ Moisten a sponge, taking care to squeeze out all the excess moisture.

☆ Load the moistened sponge by firmly rubbing it on the surface of the paint in a circular motion.

☆ Beginning with the lightest colour, apply the paint to the face starting at the centre and moving outwards. Use a combination of sweeping, dabbing and buffing motions.

☆ Using a different sponge, switch to your next colour. Blend this in the desired shape around the edges of the first colour. Don't leave ragged edges around the hair or jaw line.

☆ Remember: effective blending takes time to master and is best achieved using a barely damp sponge.

☆ Be extra careful when working near the eyes – only go as close as you are confident to. Constantly remind your model to keep their eyes closed while working near them. Do not apply glitter too close to the eyes.

☆ Keep your model steady by placing your hand on top of their head or under their chin.

Star Tips

Before you start your session moisten all your sponges. This way you need only dip the edge of your sponge into the water when required; this helps to avoid over-wetting your sponge and cuts down on mess.

BRUSHWORK

☆ Choose the right brush for the right stroke. Use a thick brush for bold strokes and a thin one for detail. Always use confident flowing strokes.

☆ Load the brush with paint. The consistency of the paint is very important for brushwork; too thin and it will run, too thick and it won't flow, causing an unsightly dragging effect.

☆ In general it's good practice to work from the top of the face downwards and to start with the lightest colour.

☆ Until you are more confident paint your weakest side first (i.e. if you are right-handed paint the left side first and vice versa).

☆ Use the side or heel of your hand to steady your brush on the model's face. This will help prevent wobbly lines.

☆ Don't overfill the face with too much busy brushwork, and when you have finished check the symmetry of your design.

☆ Different strokes can be acheived with the same brush by applying more or less pressure, turning the brush during the stroke, or by using a different side of the brush. Again practise on the back of your hand or arm.

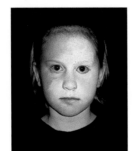

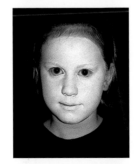

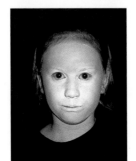

Star Tips

If you're having trouble blending, try going back to your previous sponge, and 'buff' gently on the blend line. Do not add any more water or paint.

Star Tips

Black paint is probably the most difficult to get right. Aim for a consistency just a little thicker than Indian ink. Make a little well in the bottom of your paint pot and add about four or five brushfulls of water. Gently mix in the paint.

BIG CATS
TOMMY THE TIGER

If you have a child who just won't keep still, try this simple face. It's very quick to do but the end result is very effective.

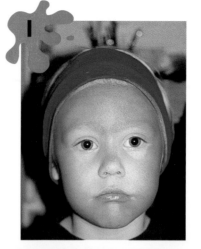

1 Apply a yellow base all over the face and blend in some orange around the outer edges of the face and down the nose.

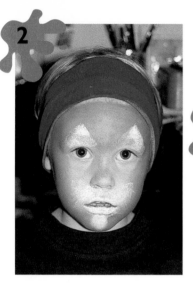

2 Using a sponge dab on some eye and muzzle shapes in white.

3 Using a medium brush and some black paint, apply eye markings, nose, whiskers and stripes, as shown.

COLOURS REQUIRED

white

black

orange

yellow

DADDY TIGER

Tommy's Dad is joining in the fun. You really can get some amazing effects with face painting and in this design we shift the features of the face to create the illusion of an open mouth. It's a little more advanced, but once you've mastered the other tigers you'll be ready to have a go at this one. Just take special care when positioning the line work.

1 Apply the base colours as on page 8, but leave the chin white. Using a thin brush, paint the outlines of the teeth in black. Note that these are positioned below the lip, on the chin. Use the photograph to help you.

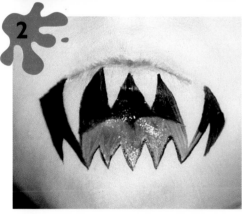

2 Now, using a medium brush, paint the tongue in red and the inside of the throat in black.

3 Using the same brush, outline the mouth in black. Complete the rest of the tiger.

SABRE TOOTH TIGER

1 Using a sponge, apply a white base over the whole face. Now blend in some yellow around the edges, avoiding the eye and mouth areas.

2 To finish the base, blend in some orange around the outer edges and down the bridge of the nose.

Star Tip

These tiger stripes are best achieved working from the outside to the inside of the face. Choose a large flat brush. Lay the brush down sideways and using a sweeping stroke, turn the brush slightly between the fingers as you move it along.

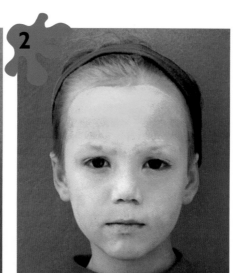

3 Using a brush, apply some white eyebrows. Start at the inside of the actual eyebrow and lay the brush down, flicking the brush up towards the outer edge of the forehead four or five times, each time moving further along the brow. Using the same brush apply more white paint to form the white tiger stripes around the face.

COLOURS REQUIRED

 white

black

orange

yellow

Star Tip

Hands and hair can be painted to match the face.

4 Clean the brush and change to black paint. Apply the black eye markings: start below the inner corner of the eye and take the line across the eyelid and underneath the eyebrow, flicking it up at the end. Then starting at the same position, this time take the line above the eyebrow and flick it across the lower part of forehead. Paint the end of the nose black. Draw a line from the centre of the nose down to the top lip. Fill the whole top lip in black and extend the mouth upwards. Paint the centre of the bottom lip in black. Leave a gap at either side for the teeth. Draw some black tiger stripes in between the existing white ones. Now switch to a thin brush and paint in the whiskers and dots. Paint the outline of the sabre teeth. Finish the tiger with a sparkle of glitter on the tip of the nose.

LEOPARD

A leopard face can be made from the same base as the tiger, so follow the same steps (omitting the stripes of course). Paint on a nose, mouth and whiskers and then, when this is complete, follow the steps below for the leopard markings.

COLOURS REQUIRED

white

black

orange

yellow

I Load the large flat brush with black paint. Starting on the bridge of the nose press the brush down gently and paint small marks up to the forehead; adding a little more pressure as you go along to get larger markings. Repeat this over the whole forehead area.

2 For the other leopard spots on the rest of the face, think of them as 'kiss' marks, with a top and bottom lip making the spots. Just flick the brush in two semi-circles opposite each other.

Star Tip
Try using metallic colours as a base on dark skin.

COLOURS REQUIRED

white

black

gold

bronze

BLACK PANTHER

For darker skins you need to consider carefully which colours and products to use. Pale colours applied directly to dark skins will appear uneven and patchy. In order to achieve an even colour you may need to use a cake make-up base first. This acts as as a kind of undercoat for the base colour. Alternatively, use darker base colours or metallic paints, which work particularly well on dark skin.

This face demonstrates the 'eyes on eyes' trick which is particularly dramatic. It can be used to great effect for all kinds of faces but works especially well on cats and monsters. Before you start you need to be sure that your model is able to keep very still and keep their eyes closed.

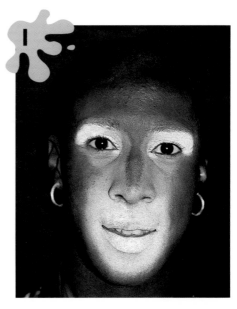

COLOURS REQUIRED

white

black

grey

yellow

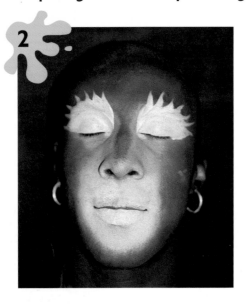

1 Apply a grey base all over the face, but avoid the eyelids. Blend in some black around the outside edges of the face and down the bridge of the nose.

2 Using a large flat brush paint in some white eyebrows and whiskers. Next paint the whole of the eyelid yellow. Remind your model to keep their eyes closed while you are painting near them.

3 Outline the eye in black and add a black iris. Now complete the nose, lips and whisker dots in black.

LUKE THE LION CUB

This is a quick and simple one for the tinies!

1 Sponge on an even gold base.

2 Sponge on some eye and muzzle shapes in white around the eyes, mouth and nose.

3 Paint in the black nose, eye markings and whisker dots. Add lots of gold glitter to give this lion cub an extra air of majesty.

COLOURS REQUIRED

white

black

gold

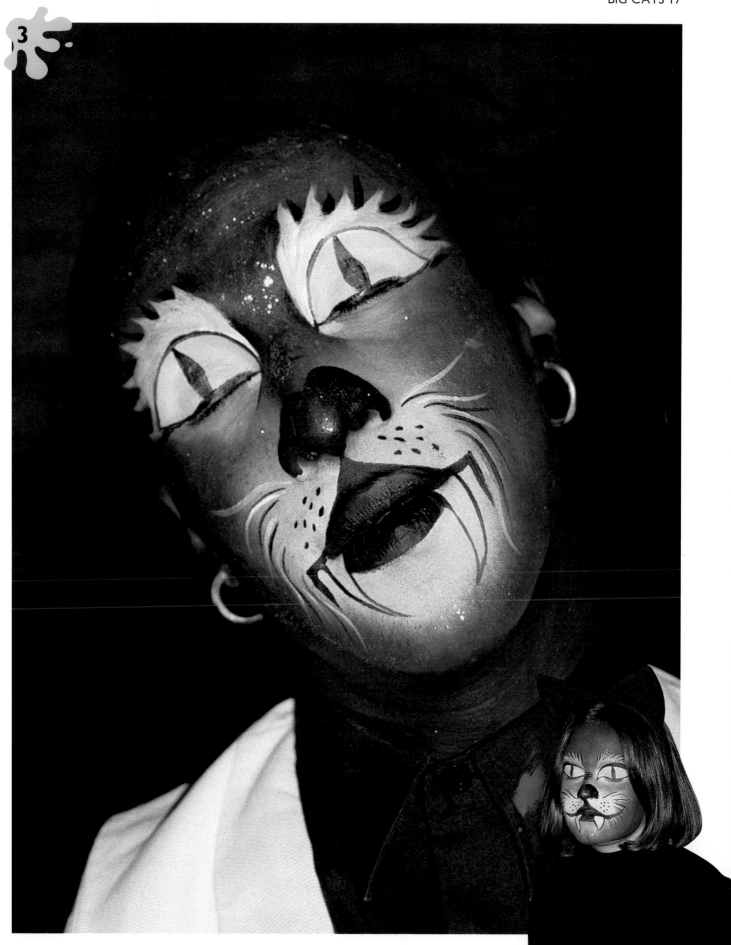

PUSSYCATS

These are always popular and easily adaptable. Try different eyebrow and whisker shapes and have fun blending colours. Also try combining metallic and normal colours for a stunning effect.

KITTY-CAT

Ideal for the wrigglers. Quick, easy and delightfully effective.

1 Apply a pale yellow base and blend in some bright pink around the outer edges of the face. 2. Using a sponge, dab on some white shapes, as eyebrows and a muzzle.

2 Paint on a red nose and lips and complete the outer face markings in royal blue, as shown in the picture below.

COLOURS REQUIRED
- white
- blue
- bright pink
- pale yellow

MOUNTAIN CAT

1 Sponge on a white muzzle and blend in some yellow over the rest of the face. Blend some orange over the forehead and then down the bridge of the nose.

2 Complete the nose, eyebrows and outer face markings in black and white.

COLOURS REQUIRED
- white
- black
- orange
- yellow

PEA-GREEN CAT

1 Apply a pale green base. Blend in some sea green around the outer edges of the face and down the bridge of the nose.

2 Highlight the cheeks with bright yellow and apply a bright pink nose and bottom lip.

3 Complete the eyebrows and outer face markings in white and black.

COLOURS REQUIRED

- white
- black
- pale green
- sea green
- yellow
- bright pink

GLAMOUR-PUSS

1 Apply an even gold base and blend in some dark red around the edge of the face and down the bridge of nose.

2 Paint on a bright pink bottom lip.

3 Complete the eyebrows and other face markings in black and white, as shown.

COLOURS REQUIRED

- white
- black
- gold
- dark red
- bright pink

CLOWNS

Clowns come in all shapes, sizes and colours, so have some fun creating your own. Below are some clowns' faces for you to try out. Remember – you're never fully dressed without a smile, so get painting!

1 Sponge on an even white base over the whole face and apply some nice bright rosy cheeks. An even white base is the most difficult to achieve, so ensure your sponge is not too wet otherwise this will lead to streaking. A white cake make-up base can be used instead of a white paint base and this is generally easier to apply evenly.

2 Paint in some contrasting colours around the eyes. All shapes will do and you can choose the colours to match the clown's clothes.

3 Give your clown a bright red nose and a happy smiley mouth. Dab a touch of glitter on the end of their nose.

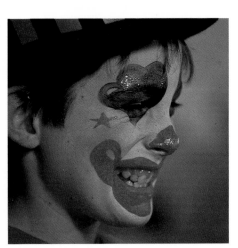

COLOURS REQUIRED

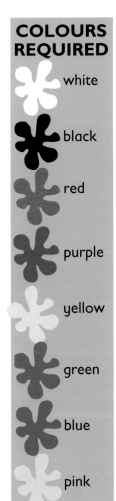

white

black

red

purple

yellow

green

blue

pink

Star Tip

When painting in the nose and mouth, leave a little of the white base peeping through. This looks like a shiny highlight.

SUGAR & SPICE AND ALL THINGS NICE...

Every little girl would like to be a princess if only for a day; with face painting you can transform any young lady into the vision of her fairytale dreams. Flowers, butterflies, stars, rainbows, the only limit is your own imagination. Ask your model for her favourite colours, for inspiration. Study the photographs carefully and practise the strokes for the different flower shapes, stars and so on. You'll be surprised how quickly you can master them.

ROSE QUEEN

1 Apply a pearly white base to the whole face and blend in some pale yellow around the outer edges. Brush on some pink blusher over the eyelids, down the cheekbones and on the chin and the forehead. This adds shading and depth.

2 Paint the roses and buds in the desired position on the face. While you've got a brush full of red paint give the model some ruby lips.

3 Using the same sized brush, add the green leaves around the roses and buds. Change to a thin brush to join the roses with thin green stems and add a few tendrils here and there.

Star Tip

For perfect petal and leaf shapes every time remember these simple guidelines:

☆ Always use a medium, rounded brush.
☆ Load your brush with paint.
☆ Choose the position of your petal/leaf.
☆ Gently put the tip of the brush down and then increase the pressure until the whole brush is in contact with the face. To make this easier, think of the brush as a foot. First put down the tip of the big toe gently and then slowly place the rest of the foot down.

4 Using the same thin brush add some depth to the roses and buds by applying some thin spirals in a dark red burgundy colour.

4

COLOURS REQUIRED

white

dark red

red

yellow

green

FLOWER PRINCESS

COLOURS REQUIRED

white

green

bright pink

yellow

1 Sponge on a white base and blend in some pink around the outer edges. Brush on blusher over the eyelids and cheekbones.

2 Using a medium brush apply five petal shapes in bright pink on either cheek and paint the lips pink. Add a yellow centre to each flower.

3 Add green eyebrows and some leaves and stems to either side of each flower.

VIOLET TIME

1 Sponge a lilac base over the whole face. Brush some pink blusher over the eyelids, down the cheeks and on the chin and forehead.

COLOURS REQUIRED

liliac

purple

pink

yellow

2 Apply some violet shapes and buds using a medium brush and purple paint. Check the symmetry of your design as you go along. Give the flowers yellow centres.

3 Fill in the gaps with some green leaves and join them up with thin, green stems. Finish the whole thing off with lipstick and glitter.

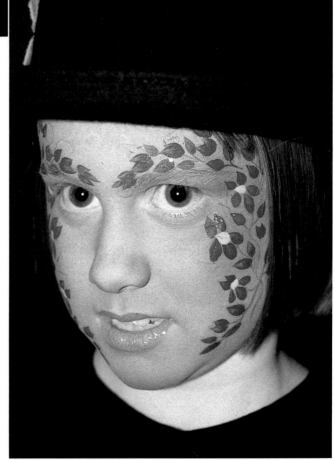

HEARTS AND FLOWERS

Combine all your different flower shapes with this delightfully pretty face.

1 Sponge on a white base, then add some blusher over the eyelids and cheekbones.

2 Paint a red heart on either cheek and one in the centre of the forehead.

3 Now arrange the various flower shapes around the hearts.

4 Finish off with some ruby lips and glitter.

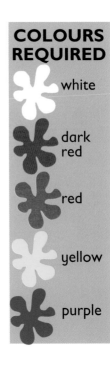

COLOURS REQUIRED

white

dark red

red

yellow

purple

DAISY MAY

Once you have mastered the various flower shapes (remember, practice makes perfect!) you can use them to great effect either individually or together. Here's a lovely summer face using the basic daisy shape.

COLOURS REQUIRED

white

green

pale green

yellow

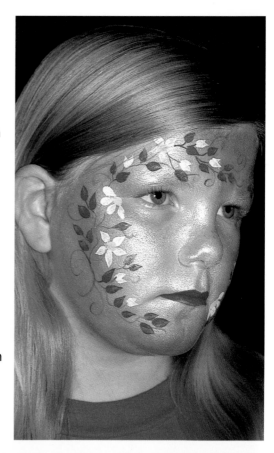

1 Sponge on a white base and blend in some pale green around the edges. (Pearly white and metallic green have been used in the photograph below.) Add some pink blusher over the eyelids, cheekbones, chin and forehead.

2 Now place some daisies, buds and leaves in a chain, around the face. Finish off with red lips and glitter.

Star Tip

It is very easy to get carried away and overfill the face, resulting in a very busy design, so try to leave the centre of the face clear. This will give you a more satisfactory end result.

STRAWBERRY PATCH

COLOURS REQUIRED

white

black

red

green

yellow

1 Sponge on a white base, blend in some pale yellow around the outer edges and brush on some pink blusher over the eyelids, cheekbones, forehead and chin. Paint on some small red hearts as shown and paint the lips while you have a red brush.

2 Now paint on some white flower shapes with yellow centres.

3 Draw some green leaves around the strawberries and flowers. With a small brush, give the strawberries their seeds and shade them on one side, with black paint to add depth. Add the green stems and fronds.

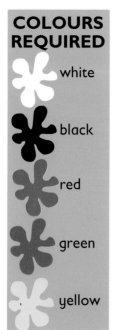

DOLLY DIMPLE

1 Sponge on an even white base and apply some blusher for large rosy cheeks.

2 Add some lilac paint around the eyes, use black for the eyebrows and eyelashes, and add some freckles in brown.

3 Finish off with red rosebud lips.

COLOURS REQUIRED

white

black

red

brown

lilac

ARABIAN PRINCESS

1 Apply a beige skin tone base and brush on some blusher.

2 Paint in some blue eyeshadow and glamorous pink lips.

3 Using a thin brush, carefully outline the eyes in black.

4 Add some glitter and a cosmetic jewel in the centre of the forehead.

COLOURS REQUIRED

beige

black

blue

pink

Star Tip

You can use a self-adhesive cosmetic jewel or the genuine theatrical variety which is stuck on with a water-based spirit gum or mastix (cosmetic glue).

NATURE'S GIFTS

Now have a go at imitating these colourful creatures and wonders found in nature.

CARNIVAL RAINBOW

This is very effective and depends on good blending to achieve the graduated rainbow effect.

Star Tip

Remember, blending is easiest when the sponge is barely damp. If you are having trouble, try going back to your previous colour/sponge and dabbing along the blend line.

1 Using a sponge, start at the top of the face and apply some purple to the whole forehead.

2 Working quickly while the purple paint is still damp, blend in some bright pink over the eye area.

3 Again, while the pink is still damp blend in some yellow around the nose and cheeks.

COLOURS REQUIRED

* pale blue
* black
* bright pink
* purple
* yellow

4 Finally, blend in some pale blue over the chin area.

5 Now, using black paint, apply some stars and swirls.

6 Finish off with pink lips, cosmetic stars and glitter.

Star Tip

Cosmetic stars come in small bottles and can be applied individually using cosmetic gel.

BUTTERFLY

COLOURS REQUIRED

white

black

orange

yellow

pink

purple

red

lilac

1 Using a large flat brush, paint in the basic shape of the butterfly as shown in the photograph. As you are going to use two other colours on the wings make sure you don't extend this first colour too far. Now apply the second colour, blending it with the first.

2 Finish the wings with a third colour, blending it into the second colour. Paint in the body of the butterfly down the nose. Using a fine brush, outline the wings with thin scallop shapes.

3 Paint in the antennae and add some swirls and leaf shapes for the wing markings. Add glitter, and watch your butterfly sparkle.

BUTTERFLIES GALORE

You can really let your imagination run wild with butterflies. Try some different wing shapes and experiment with different colours – or why not try lots of butterflies, using petal and leaf shapes for the wings. You can even mix butterflies with flowers. The sky's the limit, so have some fun!

ICE MAIDEN

COLOURS REQUIRED

white

lilac

dark blue

pale blue

1 Sponge on a white base and blend in some pale blue around the edges.

2 Paint on some snowflake shapes in white and lilac and some exaggerated blue eyebrows.

3 Decorate with cosmetic stars, jewels and lots of glitter.

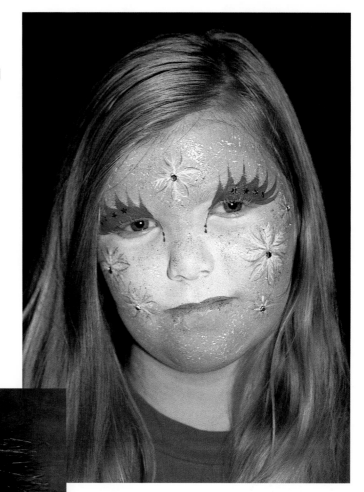

STAR QUEEN

1 Sponge on a mid-blue base and blend in some royal blue around the eyes. Add some blusher over the eyelids, cheekbones, chin and forehead.

2 Now paint in some glamorous black eyebrows and stars. Finish off with some bright pink lips, cosmetic stars and glitter for a fantastic star queen.

COLOURS REQUIRED

white

black

mid-blue

dark blue

bright pink

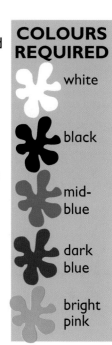

CARTOON CHARACTERS AND SUPERHEROES

Adults may not recognise these characters but the kids certainly will!

SPIDER-BOY

1 Sponge on some white paint around the eye area.

COLOURS REQUIRED

 white

black

red

2 Surround this with a red base, taking care not to go over the white eye shapes.

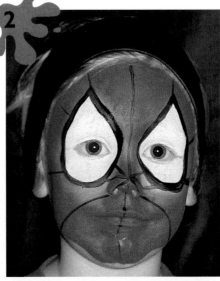

3 Using a medium brush, outline the white eye shapes in black.

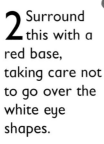

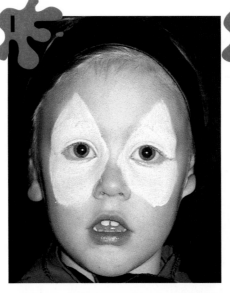

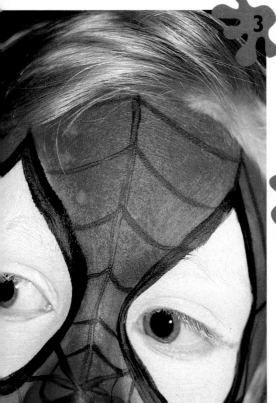

4 Switch to a fine brush and draw a line vertically down the centre of the face. Now paint another line to divide the face in half horizontally, avoiding the eye areas already painted. Next paint in two further lines to divide the face into eighths.

5 Finally, join up your web by painting 'W' shapes above the nose and 'M' shapes below it.

BATMAN

1 Sponge on a royal blue base, avoiding the eye area and leaving a clear patch in the centre of the forehead.

2 Paint on the outline of a bat in black and fill in using a large flat brush. Paint the lips black.

3 Now paint in a large yellow circle for the moon in the centre of the forehead. Finish off with some small bats flying across the moon and outline the bat wings in silver and glitter.

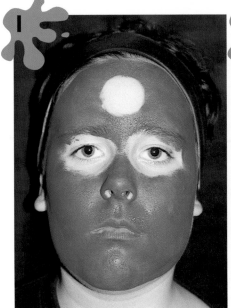

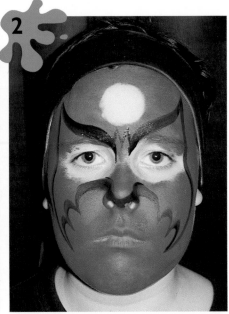

Star Tip
Try this with a yellow or gold base.

COLOURS REQUIRED

silver

black

blue

yellow

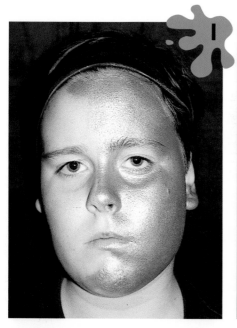

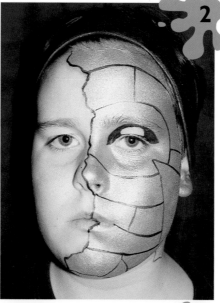

CYBORG

1 Sponge half of the face in metallic silver paint, being careful to avoid the eye.

2 Paint an outline eye shape on the eyelid in black leaving the centre blank. Paint on some robot-like plates and rivets as shown.

3 Paint a red iris in the eye outline and some dripping blood along the edge.

COLOURS REQUIRED

silver

black

red

Star Tip

Theatre blood looks so realistic and boys love it! But take care when using theatre blood as some types stain clothing.

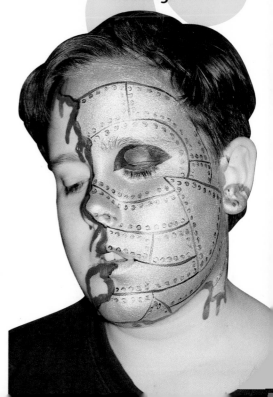

FANTASY FACES

These fantasy faces are based on sunset backgrounds and clever silhouettes. First practise your blending and then perfect your silhouettes.

MANHATTAN SKYLINE

1 Starting at the forehead sponge on a band of orange. Blend down the face through to yellow, bright pink and finishing with purple over the chin. Sponge in a yellow sun.

2 Using a large flat brush paint in some skyscraper shapes as shown. A simple body shape with an arm upraised and some spikes to represent the headress make a passable statue of liberty.

3 Using a large, almost dry brush apply some white highlights and glitter to the skyscrapers. Finish off with some bird sillouettes in black.

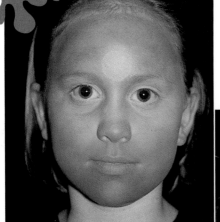

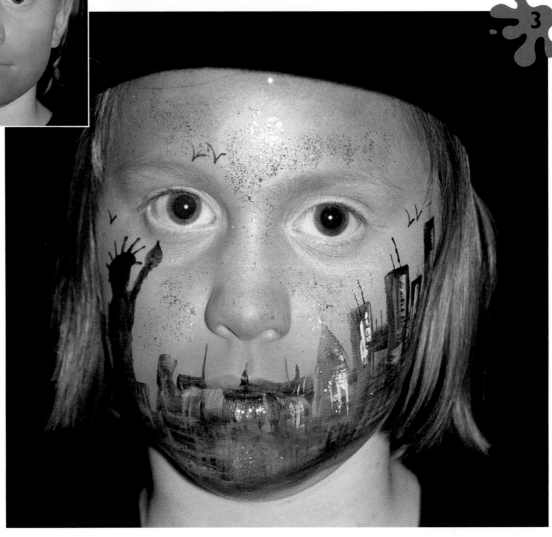

COLOURS REQUIRED

 white

 black

orange

yellow

bright pink

 purple

CARIBBEAN SUNSET

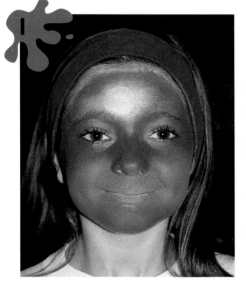

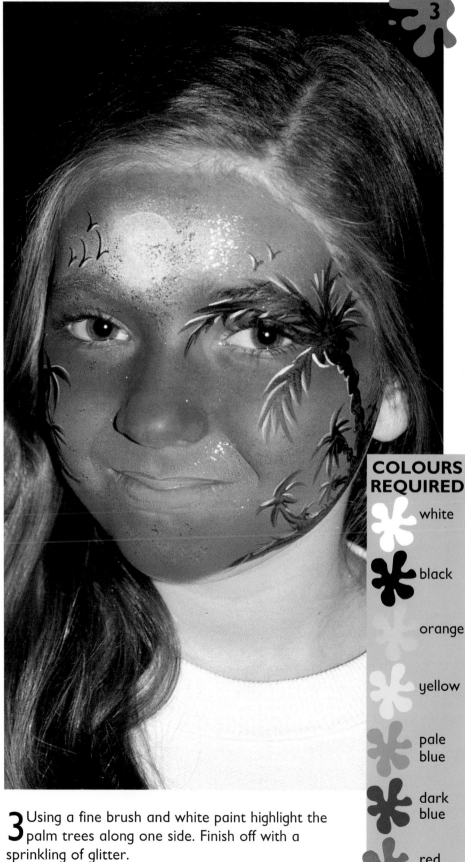

1 Starting at the forehead and working down, sponge on a band of orange, red, light blue, dark blue and sunshine yellow.

2 Paint in a large palm tree shape over one eye and add a couple more smaller palm trees around the base of the larger one. Draw the base of the island below the trees. Now paint some even smaller palm trees and another island on the other cheek, and some flying birds dotted around the face.

3 Using a fine brush and white paint highlight the palm trees along one side. Finish off with a sprinkling of glitter.

COLOURS REQUIRED

* white
* black
* orange
* yellow
* pale blue
* dark blue
* red

KISSING FISH

This is very effective as it creates the illusion of the model's teeth and mouth being those of the fish!

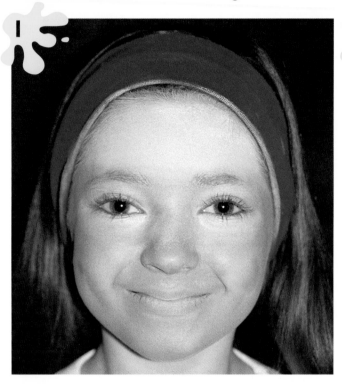

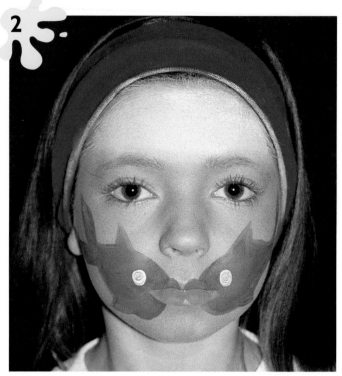

1 Sponge on a pale blue base, leaving a small patch on each cheek and the upper part of the forehead. Sponge on some white over the forehead area.

2 Paint on a fish shape in orange on either cheek as shown. Draw in some bright pink lips and paint the eyes in white.

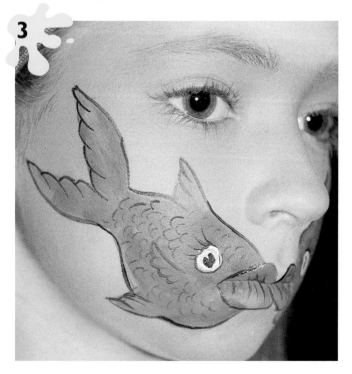

3 Using a fine brush and black paint, outline the fish; add the pupils to the eyes and scale, fin and lip detail.

4 Paint on some waves in royal blue. Finish off with glitter for a sparkly, silvery effect.

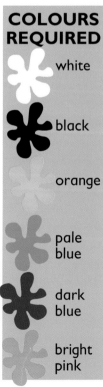

COLOURS REQUIRED

white

black

orange

pale blue

dark blue

bright pink

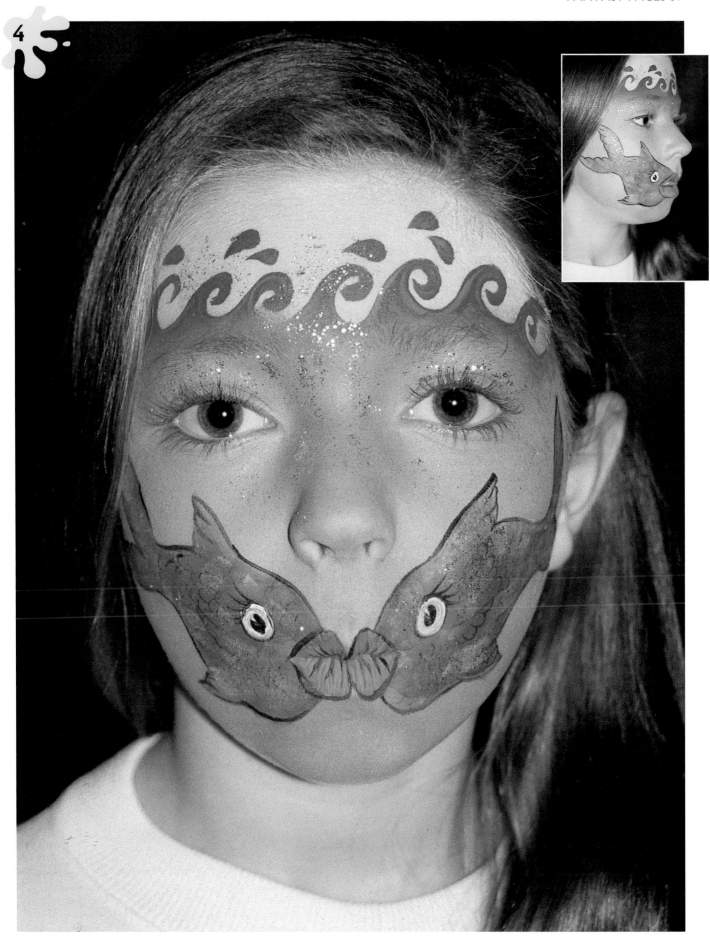

TROPICAL FISH

1 Sponge on a pale green base but leave the eyelids clear. Blend in a sea green around the edges.

2 Sponge on some bright yellow as a highlighter over the cheekbones down the nose, over the eyebrows and on the chin. Using a blusher, shade underneath the yellow highlighter on the cheek bones, forehead and chin as shown.

3 Paint in large, round yellow eyes on the eyelids and then outline them in black and draw in black pupils. Now paint the lips in bright pink and outline them in dark red. Pick out the scales in dark green and finish off with lots of glitter.

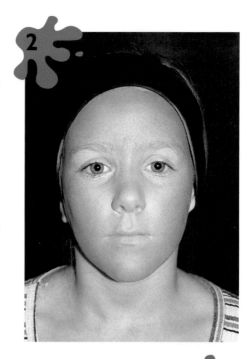

COLOURS REQUIRED

- white
- black
- yellow
- pale green
- sea green
- bright pink

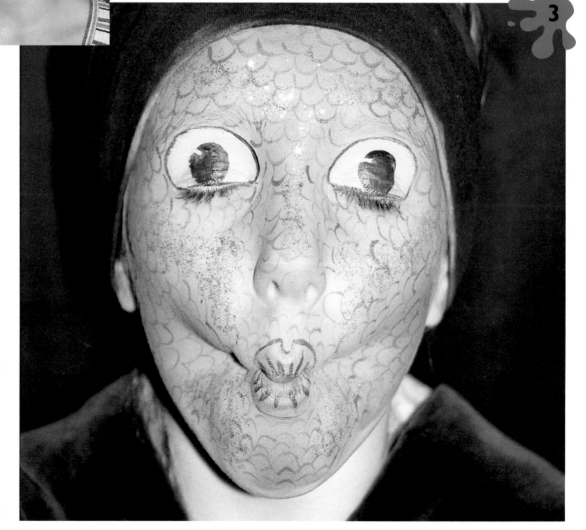

UNDER THE SEA

1 Sponge on a pale blue base over the lower half of the face and blend in some white over the top half.

2 Stipple on some white over the whole face.

3 Paint a red crab on one cheek and a pink sea horse on the other.

4 Add some seaweed.

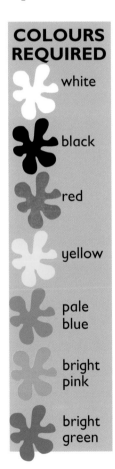

COLOURS REQUIRED

* white

* black

* red

* yellow

* pale blue

* bright pink

* bright green

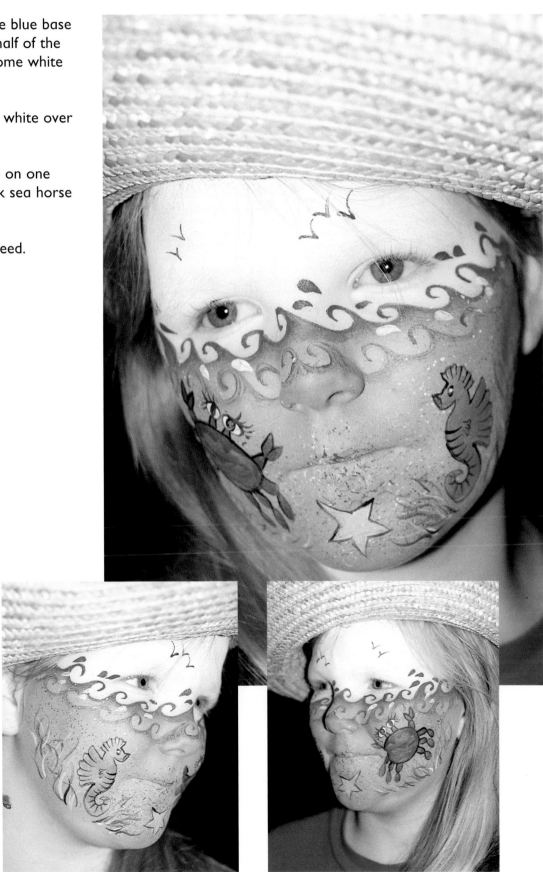

TRICK OR TREAT

Hallowe'en is a very important date in every child's calendar. It's an excuse for fancy dress parties, trick or treating and just plain devilish fun! With face painting and a bit of imaginative dressing up you can transform your kids into the monsters they truly are!

PUMPKIN HEAD

1 Apply white eye and mouth shapes as shown in the photograph. Outline these shapes in orange and black.

2 Complete the black line work.

COLOURS REQUIRED

silver

black

orange

RED DEVIL

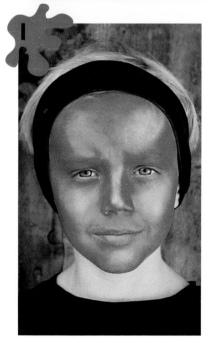

1 Apply an even gold base and sponge on some red over the top. Shade as shown using dark red.

2 Outline the eyes and add the eyebrows, moustache and beard as shown.

3 Finish off with lots of gold glitter.

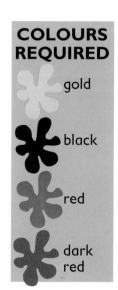

COLOURS REQUIRED

gold

black

red

dark red

Star Tip
You can buy stick-on horns from any good fancy dress outlet.

3

GREEN WITCH

COLOURS REQUIRED

yellow

black

pale green

dark green

1 Sponge on a pale green base and then blend in some dark green around the outside. Highlight with fluorescent yellow and shade with blusher.

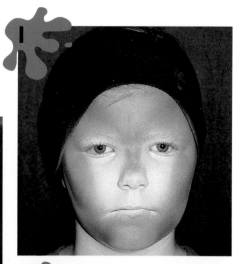

2 Apply some jagged eyebrows in black, as shown.

3 Using a fine brush paint in the web lines and the spider. Finally, apply silver glitter along each web strand.

BLUE FIEND

1 Sponge on some white over the eyes and mouth as shown. Apply a pale blue base and blend in some dark blue around the outer edges.

2 Paint some green irises on the eyelids. Add some black pupils. Outline the eyes and paint the eyebrows as shown.

3 Complete the other facial markings and outline the teeth.

COLOURS REQUIRED

white

black

pale blue

blue

T-REX

1 Sponge on some white shapes as shown and sponge some green around these shapes.

2 Using a fine brush, paint in the outline of the teeth in black (notice that the upper teeth are above the top lip and the lower teeth are on the chin).

3 Using a medium brush, paint in the irises and fill in between the teeth with red.

4 Finally, outline the eyes and mouth and paint in the nostrils, eyebrows, irises and scales.

COLOURS REQUIRED

white

black

green

red

JURASSIC SKELETON

1 Sponge on a layered base in yellow, orange and red.

2 Paint in a black skeleton head over the eye as shown.

3 Finish the rest of the skeleton. Add a thick black outline around the face.

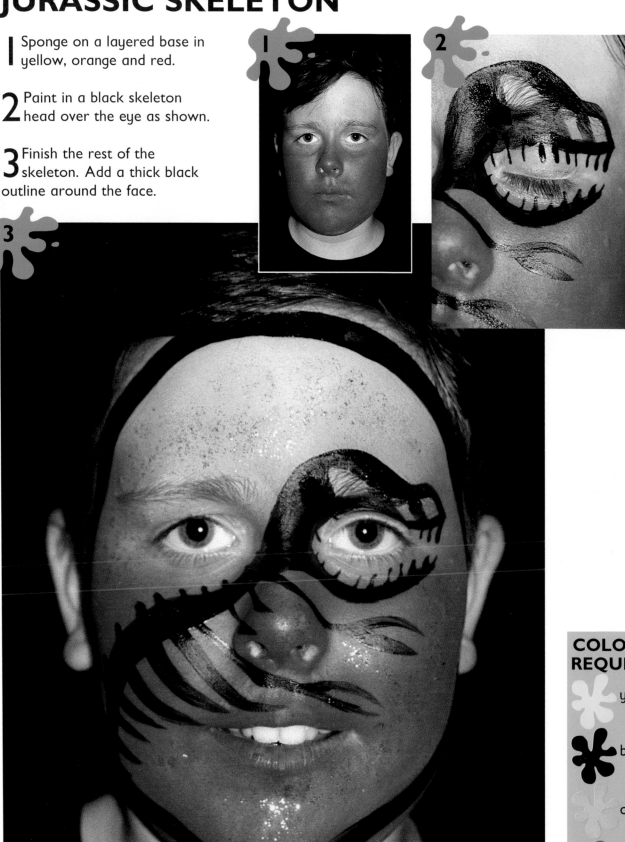

COLOURS REQUIRED

yellow

black

orange

red

VAMPIRE QUEEN

COLOURS REQUIRED

* white
* black
* grey
* red

1 Sponge on a white base and shade with grey as shown.

2 Outline the eyes in red and then outline them in black. Apply some spikey eyebrows and red lips, leaving a gap for the teeth.

3 Finally outline the teeth.

Star Tip

For a truly dramatic effect, dribble some theatrical blood from the teeth.